Galatians

Annotated

Whitecaps Media
Houston

Whitecaps Media
Houston, Texas
www.whitecapsmedia.com

Galatians, Annotated
© *2009 by Kit Sublett. All rights reserved.*

For information on bulk sales, contact Whitecaps Media at the above address or by email at whitecapsmedia@earthlink.net

ISBN 13: 978-0-9758577-8-6

Printed in the United States

Dedicated to my mom

Ruth Allyn Whitlock Sublett

whose own example of unconditional love and grace
made it easy for all of her children to believe in God's

❧

Introduction

Galatians is a small book—only about 3,200 words in the English Standard Version—but it is one of the most powerful in all of Scripture. It provides some of the clearest doctrine in all of the Bible. The basic premise is that we are saved by faith, not by works. The idea is not unique to Galatians, of course, but Galatians spells out the argument irrefutably.

In 1521, Philip Melanchton in his book *Common Topics*, wrote, "Of the whole of Scripture there are two parts: the law and the gospel. The law indicates the sickness, the gospel the remedy." This is nowhere more clearly expressed than in Galatians.

Galatians was Martin Luther's favorite book in the Bible and his study of it led him to begin the Protestant Reformation. (I have even heard it said that he referred to Galatians as his wife!) Numerous church leaders including John and Charles Wesley (the brothers who founded the Methodist movement) trace their own salvation to studying Paul's diminutive masterpiece.

Henrietta Mears summed up Paul's preaching on grace this way: "It has been said that Judaism was the cradle of Christianity and very nearly its grave. God raised up Paul as the Moses of the Christian church to deliver them from this bondage." As you become familiar with Paul's letter to the Galatians, you will understand more fully why Miss Mears made this bold statement.

In my notes I have tried to add clarity to the verses without getting in the way. I have also tried to "interpret Scripture by Scripture," showing how God's Word is a unified whole with a consistent message.

How to Use This Book

This book has four parts: the entire book of Galatians in the English Standard Version (ESV) along with my annotations; Appendix A, which is the book of Galatians in the ESV without my commentary; Appendix B, which is the King James Version (KJV) of the book; and Appendix C, which contains study questions for group discussion or individual study.

I suggest you first read the entire book of Galatians without the annotations (Appendix A). If you do this in one sitting you will get a better idea for the overall feel of Paul's letter. There is room for your own notes as you read along.

I'm a big believer in reading multiple translations so I also recommend you read Galatians in one of the many other excellent translations out there. The KJV text is included in this book as a comparison. While the KJV is not easy to understand, it can give you different insights to the text.

Second, read Galatians and my annotations. In these notes I have tried to add clarity to the verses without getting in the way. I have also tried to "interpret Scripture by Scripture," showing how God's Word is a unified whole with a consistent message. To help do this I have quoted the verses I reference, rather than make you look them up on your own (unless the reference is to a particularly long passage).

Lastly, the Study Section can be used in your own personal study or if you are studying Galatians in a group.

Paul's Letter to the

Galatians
annotated

---

1 Paul, an apostle—not from men nor through man, but through Jesus Christ and God the Father, who raised him from the dead—

² and all the brothers who are with me, ❡ To the churches of Galatia:

³ ❡ Grace to you and peace from God our Father and the Lord Jesus Christ,

⁴ who gave himself for our sins to deliver us from the present evil age,

Notes on Chapter 1

Chapter Summary This chapter sets up the theme of the book—the Gospel of Grace. Paul also defends his credentials as an apostle.

1. Paul Jim Rayburn called Paul the greatest man who ever lived, apart from Jesus, and with good reason. Rayburn's affection for Paul was due in large part to Paul's clear proclamation of the gospel of grace, seen most clearly in Romans, and also here in Galatians.

an apostle Paul describes his apostleship in 1 Corinthians 15:8–10: "Last of all, as to one untimely born, he appeared also to me. For I am the least of the apostles, unworthy to be called an apostle, because I persecuted the church of God. But by the grace of God I am what I am, and his grace toward me was not in vain. On the contrary, I worked harder than any of them, though it was not I, but the grace of God that is with me."

who raised him from the dead It is clear from reading other passages in addition to this one that it was God who raised Christ from the dead. Acts 2:24 reads, "God raised him up, loosing the pangs of death, because it was not possible for him to be held by it." Acts 4:10 says, "Let it be known to all of you and to all the people of Israel that by the name of Jesus Christ of Nazareth, whom you crucified, whom God raised from the dead . . ." Furthermore, Acts 10:40 tells us ". . . but God raised him on the third day and made him to appear . . ." Lastly, the much-quoted Romans 10:9 says, ". . . because, if you confess with your mouth that Jesus is Lord and believe in your heart that God raised him from the dead, you will be saved." Often, American Christians say "Christ rose from the dead," when it would be more accurate to say, "God raised Christ from the dead."

2. and all the brothers Paul often mentioned other people in his introductions to his letters, though it is clearly his voice in all of them.

3. Every one of Paul's thirteen letters in the New Testament contains a salutation with the dynamic duo of "grace" and "peace." Paul uses *charis* (Greek for "grace") over 100 times in his thirteen letters. A good definition for "grace" is an acronym: God's Riches at Christ's Expense. The word truly sums up Paul's doctrine of salvation.

Peace is more than the absence of war; one side must be vanquished. Peace with God does not come because God declares a "cease fire" or decides to ignore our sin. It comes because God has vanquished sin and we declare our guilt and receive His grace.

according to the will of our God and Father,

5 to whom be the glory forever and ever. Amen.

6 ¶ I am astonished that you are so quickly deserting him who called you in the grace of Christ and are turning to a different gospel—

7 not that there is another one, but there are some who trouble you and want to distort the gospel of Christ.

8 But even if we or an angel from heaven should preach to you a gospel contrary to the one we preached to you, let him be accursed.

9 As we have said before, so now I say again: If anyone is preaching to you a gospel contrary to the one you received, let him be accursed.

10 ¶ For am I now seeking the approval of man, or of God? Or am I trying to please man? If I were still trying to please man, I would not be a servant of Christ.

11 ¶ For I would have you know, brothers, that

---

4. This verse says much about Christ and His sacrifice: it was voluntary ("who gave himself"), it was because of us ("for our sins"), and it was God's will ("according to the will of our God and Father"). Notice that in this one verse Paul describes the role of each of the three major parties involved in the transaction on the cross: it was because of us, Christ performed His act of sacrifice willingly, and God the Father willed it.

6. a different gospel Different than the gospel of the grace of Christ, already partially described in verse 4 and soon to be described in greater detail. In only the sixth verse, Paul is taking a strong stand for grace.

7. there are some who trouble you There is agreement among scholars that Paul is referring here to a group known as Judaizers. Their goal was to keep Christianity a subset of Juadiasm, where Christians had to keep the Jewish Law.

[who] went to distort the gospel What was true then continues to be true today: there are still people who want to counterfeit the gospel, and it's always the same counterfeit: that you can earn your way to God! The counterfeit appeals to man's basic sin condition of pride—I can do it!

8–9. Paul uses the Greek word *anathema*, from which we get our word "anathema" (yes, it's the exact same!). The Greek word's meaning was to be set aside for eternal condemnation. The fact that Paul repeats himself in verse 9 indicates that he did not say this lightheartedly, but advisedly.

10. If I were still trying to please man We should always and only seek to please an audience of One! But that may cost us, as this verse indicates. Sometimes pleasing God will result in our making decisions that do not please others.

11. the gospel Paul uses the Greek word *euangelion* or its variants sixty times in his epistles, most of the time to describe his (Paul's) message. The word itself (used by others in the New Testament in addition to Paul) was "already in the gospel that was preached by me is not man's gospel.

12 For I did not receive it from any man, nor was I taught it, but I received it through a revelation of Jesus Christ.

13 For you have heard of my former life in Judaism, how I persecuted the church of God violently and tried to destroy it.

14 And I was advancing in Judaism beyond many of my own age among my people, so extremely zealous was I for the traditions of my fathers.

15 But when he who had set me apart before I was born, and who called me by his grace,

16 was pleased to reveal his Son to me, in order that I might preach him among the Gentiles, I did not immediately consult with anyone;

17 nor did I go up to Jerusalem to those who were apostles before me, but I went away into Arabia, and returned again to Damascus.

---

use in the Roman world," according to Mounce. "It referred to an announcement of 'glad tidings' regarding a birthday, rise to power, or decree of the emperor that was to herald the fulfillment of hopes for peace and well-being in all the world." Paul's frequent use of the term is yet another indication of the idea that he viewed the Christian message to be one based on God's doing, not man's, and therefore something to be declared and enjoyed, not earned.

not man's gospel As I stated in the notes on verse 7, man's gospel revolves around him being the star, not Him being the star!

13. You have heard of my former life Paul's earlier life is discussed in Acts 8:1–3 ("And Saul approved of [Stephen's] execution. And there arose on that day a great persecution against the church in Jerusalem, and they were all scattered throughout the regions of Judea and Samaria, except the apostles. Devout men buried Stephen and made great lamentation over him. But Saul was ravaging the church, and entering house after house, he dragged off men and women and committed them to prison."), and his conversion story is told in Acts 9:1–18.

16. I did not consult with anyone The inference here is that Paul's theology came from God directly, not from other people. This was important to Paul's accreditation as an apostle. See v. 1: "Paul, an apostle—not from men nor through man, but through Jesus Christ and God the Father..."

17. but I went away into Arabia What is now present-day Saudi Arabia and Yemen. Zondervan CBD puts this time of Paul's life between Acts 9:22 ("But Saul increased all the more in strength, and confounded the Jews who lived in Damascus by proving that Jesus was the Christ.") and Acts 9:23 ("When many days had passed, the Jews plotted to kill him."). The exact time period is not known, other than the Acts 9:23 comment that "many days had passed." The Reformation Study Bible says it was the three years mentioned in the next verse.

His motivation for going to Arabia is probably revealed earlier in the sentence when he says God called him to "preach him among the Gentiles" (verse 16).

18 ¶ Then after three years I went up to Jerusalem to visit Cephas and remained with him fifteen days.

19 But I saw none of the other apostles except James the Lord's brother.

20 (In what I am writing to you, before God, I do not lie!)

21 Then I went into the regions of Syria and Cilicia.

22 And I was still unknown in person to the churches of Judea that are in Christ.

23 They only were hearing it said, "He who used to persecute us is now preaching the faith he

---

18. Then after three years The actual amount of time could be as little as a year and a few months. Halley says that Jews had a practice of calling something a whole year when it really was only part of a year. Another example of this practice would be the expression that Jesus was dead for three days, when in reality he died in the afternoon on Friday, and arose early in the morning on Sunday.

I would add that we practice this today, as well, for instance when a high school senior says he's been in high school for four years even though it's only the beginning of his fourth year.

While Paul was probably often in solitude, it is very likely that he was spending his time preaching Christ among the Gentiles (as explained in verses 15 and 16).

Cephas Simon's nickname in Aramaic, given to him by Christ in John 1:42 ("He brought him to Jesus. Jesus looked at him and said, 'So you are Simon the son of John? You shall be called Cephas' (which means Peter).") I am not sure why Paul insists in using "Cephas" here and also 2:9, 11, and 14, but uses the Greek form "Peter" in 2:7 and 8. Both the ESV and the New American Standard Bible (NASB) have this construction, and it is the literal interpretation, while some other translations transliterate it to Peter.

to visit Cephas Barnes (citing the Greek word used) and Ryrie both comment that this visit was not to confer with Peter, but to get acquainted with each other. Whatever the motive, it was clearly a good idea for these two architects of the Christian church to meet.

Dr. Knox Chamblin notes that in Paul's recap of Jesus' post-resurrection appearances in 1 Corinthians 15, the only two eyewitnesses mentioned by name ("he appeared to Cephas, then to the twelve," 15:5; and "he appeared to James, then to all the apostles," 15:7) are the same two Paul mentions here by name in this paragraph. This might be a reflection of Paul's two weeks with Paul and what the three men (Peter, James, and Paul) talked about.

19. James the Lord's brother Jesus had a large family. Matthew 13:55 tells us that he had at least four brothers ("Is not this the carpenter's son? Is not his mother called Mary? And are not his brothers James and Joseph and Simon and Judas?"). Furthermore, in an almost identical verse, Mark 6:3 mentions that He had at least two sisters: "Is not this the carpenter, the son of Mary and brother of James and Joses and Judas and Simon? And are not his sisters here with us?" So, Mary and Joseph had at least seven children in their family: five boys (one of them Jesus) and at least two girls, perhaps more.

James is mentioned twice later in this book: 2:9 ("and when James and Cephas and John, who seemed to be pillars, perceived the grace that was given to me, they gave the right hand of fellowship to Barnabas and me, that we should go once tried to destroy."

²⁴ And they glorified God because of me.

_____

_____

_____

_____

2⁵ Then after fourteen years I went up again to Jerusalem with Barnabas, taking Titus along with me.

_____

_____

_____

_____

² I went up because of a revelation and set before them (though privately before those who seemed influential) the gospel that I proclaim among the Gentiles, in order to make sure I was not running or had not run in vain.

_____

_____

_____

_____

---

to the Gentiles and they to the circumcised.") and 2:12 ("For before certain men came from James, [Cephas] was eating with the Gentiles; but when they came he drew back and separated himself, fearing the circumcision party.")

Though there are four men in the New Testament named James, this James is believed by most to be the author of the New Testament book of that name, although that is not certain.

24. And they glorified God because of me While it may sound like bragging to our sensitive 21st century hearing, what Paul says happened should be our aim as well: that people should glorify God because of us.

Notes on Chapter 2

Chapter Summary In verses 1–10, Paul is in Jerusalem and successfully defends the doctrine of justification by faith. The second half of the chapter, verses 11–21, Paul is in Antioch, defending his message by rebuking the visiting apostle Peter.

1. Then after fourteen years Henry Halley in HBH says that the fourteen years include the three years mentioned in 1:18 ("Then after three years I went up to Jerusalem to visit Cephas and remained with him fifteen days."). It is the considered opinion of scholars that this time was one of study and meditation.

The _NIV Study Bible_ says it was probably fourteen years after Saul's conversion, which would make him in his early–mid-forties.

I went up again to Jerusalem Many think this is the trip Paul took that is recorded in Acts 11:27–30: "Now in these days prophets came down from Jerusalem to Antioch. And one of them named Agabus stood up and foretold by the Spirit that there would be a great famine over all the world (this took place in the days of Claudius). So the disciples determined, everyone according to his ability, to send relief to the brothers living in Judea. And they did so, sending it to the elders by the hand of Barnabas and Saul." Saul here being Paul.

Barnabas Also known as Joseph. We first see him in Acts 4:36–37 ("Thus Joseph, who was also called by the apostles Barnabas (which means son of encouragement), a Levite, a native of Cyprus, sold a field that belonged to him and brought the money and laid it at the apostles' feet.")

Titus The same Titus for whom the epistle is named. One of Paul's favorites (Titus 1:4: "To Titus, my true child in a common faith: Grace and peace from God the Father and Christ Jesus our Savior.").

2. Much is interesting about this verse: 1. Paul felt it best to run his message by the church leaders in Jerusalem. 2. He first met privately with some of them, a wise and calculated move. 3. He acknowledges not that others _were_ influential, but that they _seemed_ influential. He discusses this in no uncertain terms in verse 6 ("And from those who seemed to be influential (what they were makes no difference to me; God shows no partiality)—those, I say, who seemed influential

_____
_____
_____
_____

3 But even Titus, who was with me, was not forced to be circumcised, though he was a Greek.

4 Yet because of false brothers secretly brought in—who slipped in to spy out our freedom that we have in Christ Jesus, so that they might bring us into slavery—

5 to them we did not yield in submission even for a moment, so that the truth of the gospel might be preserved for you.

6 And from those who seemed to be influential (what they were makes no difference to me; God shows no partiality)—those, I say, who seemed influential added nothing to me.

7 On the contrary, when they saw that I had been entrusted with the gospel to the uncircumcised, just as Peter had been entrusted with the gospel to the circumcised

8 (for he who worked through Peter for his apostolic ministry to the circumcised worked also through me for mine to the Gentiles),

9 and when James and Cephas and John, who seemed to be pillars, perceived the grace that

---

added nothing to me.")

3. not forced to be circumcised This was important as an outward symbol of Paul's message of salvation by grace alone, and not by acts of worship or ceremony such as circumcision. The fact that Titus was not made to be circumcised spelled out the success of Paul's agenda.

4. slavery Paul's no-holds-barred description of a non-grace oriented gospel.

5. the truth of the gospel In contrast to the slavery mentioned in the previous verse, this refers to salvation solely by faith.

the truth of the gospel might be preserved for you Paul's gift to Christendom!

6. God shows no partiality Reminiscent of Romans 2:11: "For God shows no partiality." James 2:1 tells us we are to follow suit: "My brothers, show no partiality as you hold the faith in our Lord Jesus Christ, the Lord of glory."

added nothing to me Again Paul asserts his apostleship.

9. Cephas Simon's nickname in Aramaic, given to him by Christ in John 1:42 ("He brought him to Jesus. Jesus looked at him and said, 'So you are Simon the son of John? You shall be called Cephas' (which means Peter)."). I am not sure why Paul insists in using "Cephas" here and also 1:18, 2:11 and 14, but uses the Greek form "Peter" in 2:7 and 8. Both the ESV and the NASB have this construction, and it is the literal interpretation, while some other translations transliterate was given to me, they gave the right hand of fellowship to Barnabas and me, that we should go to the Gentiles and they to the circumcised.

¹⁰ Only, they asked us to remember the poor, the very thing I was eager to do.

¹¹ ¶ But when Cephas came to Antioch, I opposed him to his face, because he stood condemned.

¹² For before certain men came from James, he was eating with the Gentiles; but when they came he drew back and separated himself, fearing the circumcision party.

¹³ And the rest of the Jews acted hypocritically along with him, so that even Barnabas was led astray by their hypocrisy.

¹⁴ But when I saw that their conduct was not in step with the truth of the gospel, I said to Cephas before them all, "If you, though a Jew, live like a Gentile and not like a Jew, how can you force the Gentiles to live like Jews?"

---

it to Peter.

seemed to be pillars It is possible that Paul is saying this ironically, along the lines of "the governor and the president, who seemed to be important …", stating the obvious in an ironic way. Or it might be genuine sarcasm because both Cephas (through his actions described only a few verses later in 11–14) and James (possibly in v. 12) showed weakness (as opposed to the strength of pillars) after originally backing the doctrine of justification by faith.

10. the very thing I was eager to do Paul's message wasn't just about grace. He also felt strongly about "remembering the poor."

11. Though Peter may have been slow to come around to the gospel of grace, he eventually did and certainly had fully embraced it by the time he wrote 1 and 2 Peter.

I opposed him to his face Paul is one gutsy dude! Given Martin Luther's admiration for this book, I wonder if Paul's resolution in this circumstance provided the great reformer with inspiration as he stood up to the authorities of his day 1500 years later.

12. certain men came from James Does this mean James was backing off of his stance in verse 9 ("and when James and Cephas and John, who seemed to be pillars, perceived the grace that was given to me, they gave the right hand of fellowship to Barnabas and me …")? Is that why he only seemed like a pillar? Or was it just a reflection of Peter's wimpiness, that is, once these guys showed up that he knew from back home, he gave in to peer pressure? In any case, Paul was understandably upset.

13. even Barnabas was led astray by their hypocricy It would appear that Paul was really on his own here.

14–21. Paul's rebuke of Peter.

14. But when I saw their conduct was not in step with the truth of the gospel Paul was willing to risk

¹⁵ We ourselves are Jews by birth and not Gentile sinners;

¹⁶ yet we know that a person is not justified by works of the law but through faith in Jesus Christ, so we also have believed in Christ Jesus, in order to be justified by faith in Christ and not by works of the law, because by works of the law no one will be justified.

¹⁷ But if, in our endeavor to be justified in Christ, we too were found to be sinners, is Christ then a servant of sin? Certainly not!

¹⁸ For if I rebuild what I tore down, I prove myself to be a transgressor.

¹⁹ For through the law I died to the law, so that I might live to God.

²⁰ I have been crucified with Christ. It is no lon-

---

fellowship for the sake of the essential truth of the gospel. It is good to see that Peter took it well. Years after the confrontation, Peter wrote in 2 Peter 3:15–16, "And count the patience of our Lord as salvation, just as our beloved brother Paul also wrote to you according to the wisdom given him, as he does in all his letters when he speaks in them of these matters. There are some things in them that are hard to understand, which the ignorant and unstable twist to their own destruction, as they do the other Scriptures." The importance here is twofold: he refers to Paul as a beloved brother, and also refers to Paul's writings as Scripture. (On a side note, I appreciate Peter finding some of Paul's writings "hard to understand," since I do, too!)

It is perhaps the natural order of man to continually be "sucked into" a performance mentality and run back to what Paul calls slavery (v. 4: "Yet because of false brothers secretly brought in—who slipped in to spy out our freedom that we have in Christ Jesus, so that they might bring us into slavery . . .")

16. A summation of Paul's doctrine of grace. Three times in this one verse he repeats the idea of faith over works.

17–18. Here's what I think he's saying: if we sin after placing our trust in Christ (and therefore having become Christians according to the gospel of grace), does that make Christ a servant of sin? No. Indeed, if a believer returns to the law as a vehicle of salvation ("rebuild what I tore down") it would not have the power to save him, and only condemns him as a transgressor.

18. what I tore down The idea of salvation by works. And if he "rebuilds" it, that means he (or anyone else who does so) is guilty of sin. That's my interpretation. Some believe Paul is saying that if a Christian sins, he is still condemned by the law. In other words, Christ does not promote unrighteousness.

19. For through the law I died to the law Reminiscent of Romans 7:4 ("Likewise, my brothers, you also have died to the law through the body of Christ, so that you may belong to another, to him who has been raised from the dead, in order that we may bear fruit for God").

J. B. Phillips translates verse 19 as, "For under the Law I 'died,' and I am dead to the Law's demands so that I may live for God." We die to the law so we may live for someone else—God.

20. It is no longer I who live This is consistent with 2 Cor. 5:15 ("and he died for all, that those who live might no ger I who live, but Christ who lives in me. And the life I now live in the flesh I live by faith in the Son of God, who loved me and gave himself for me.

²¹ I do not nullify the grace of God, for if justification were through the law, then Christ died for no purpose.

3 ¦ O FOOLISH GALATIANS! Who has bewitched you? It was before your eyes that Jesus Christ was publicly portrayed as crucified.

² Let me ask you only this: Did you receive the

---

longer live for themselves but for him who for their sake died and was raised.")

the Son of God, who loved me and gave himself for me This sounds so 21st century to me! This verse echoes Paul's sentiment in Romans 6:6: "We know that our old self was crucified with him in order that the body of sin might be brought to nothing, so that we would no longer be enslaved to sin."

21. Yet another strong statement Paul makes about grace.

Notes on Chapter 3
Chapter Summary I find this chapter very difficult to understand in the ESV, so I have undertaken to paraphrase it in this summary. This is what I believe Paul is saying:

Don't believe another gospel. The gospel gave you the Spirit—no other "gospel" could do that.

And now you are trying to do by yourself what the Spirit has begun and must complete—making you Christlike.

No, it's all about belief and faith, just like it was for Abraham.

It is faith that truly connects us to Abraham, not blood lineage.

Meanwhile, those who try to save themselves by being good are cursed.

Nope. Faith is the key. Faith in Christ, who obeyed the law perfectly and then cancelled the law.

Here's the deal with the law: it came 430 years after the promise to Abraham of Christ (which promise Abraham received by believing). No, our inheritance as sons of God comes through believing in Christ as Abraham did, not through the law. The promise came before the law and supersedes it.

So why do we even have the law? It was a stopgap measure until Christ came along to complete the picture.

But now the picture is complete—we have Christ! Now we, like Abraham, are God's children. This is not by birth or blood or ceremony but by faith.

1. 0 foolish Galatians He has finished reporting on his confrontation with the apostles and is now directly addressing the Christians of Galatia.

Who has bewitched you? The definition of "bewitched" is "to cast a spell over."

2. We receive the Holy Spirit upon our conversion (Ephesians 1:13–14: "In him you also, when you heard the word of truth, the gospel of your salvation, and believed in him, were sealed with the promised Holy Spirit, who is the guarantee of our inheritance until we acquire possession of it, to the praise of his glory."). Here Paul puts forth yet another argu-

Spirit by works of the law or by hearing with faith?

3 Are you so foolish? Having begun by the Spirit, are you now being perfected by the flesh?

4 Did you suffer so many things in vain—if indeed it was in vain?

5 Does he who supplies the Spirit to you and works miracles among you do so by works of the law, or by hearing with faith—

6 just as Abraham "believed God, and it was counted to him as righteousness"?

7 Know then that it is those of faith who are the sons of Abraham.

8 And the Scripture, foreseeing that God would

---

ment for grace by observing that the Spirit is received through faith, not through works.

4. Did you suffer so many things in vain Acts 14:1–7; 21–22 indicate that the churches in Galatia had suffered persecution. This may very well be the suffering Paul is referring to in this verse.

5. works miracles among you . . . by hearing with faith Miracles come as a result of faith, not good works. Jesus' healing miracles are demonstrations of this. An excellent example is the healing of the cenurion's servant in Luke 7. Though others told Jesus that the centurion deserved to have his servant healed, the centurion himself claimed no such honor, trusting instead only in Jesus' mercy.

hearing with faith This phrase is reminiscent of Romans 10:17: "So faith comes from hearing, and hearing through the word of Christ."

6. A citation of Genesis 15:6: "And he believed the Lord, and he counted it to him as righteousness." Paul also cites Genesis 15:6 in Romans 4:3 ("For what does the Scripture say? 'Abraham believed God, and it was counted to him as righteousness'").

Using Abraham is significant, since circumcision came through Abraham (Genesis 17:9–11: "And God said to Abraham, 'As for you, you shall keep my covenant, you and your offspring after you throughout their generations. This is my covenant, which you shall keep, between me and you and your offspring after you: Every male among you shall be circumcised. You shall be circumcised in the flesh of your foreskins, and it shall be a sign of the covenant between me and you.'")

In the book of Galatians, circumcision is the picture of the Law. Paul's point is that circumcision itself does not negate grace—it is a physical reminder of God's covenant to Abraham which was all about faith. The inability of circumcision to save is perhaps shown by its male-only nature.

Just as Abraham Even though circumcision came through Abraham, he himself was not justified by circumcision, but through faith (Genesis 15:6: "And he believed the Lord, and he counted it to him as righteousness").

7. This verse is reminiscent of John 1:12: "But to all who did receive him, who believed in his name, he gave the right to become children of God."

8. A citation of Genesis 12:3: "I will bless those who bless you, and him who dishonors you I will curse, and in you all the families of the earth shall be blessed."

justify the Gentiles by faith, preached the gospel beforehand to Abraham, saying, "In you shall all the nations be blessed."

⁹ So then, those who are of faith are blessed along with Abraham, the man of faith.

¹⁰ ⁋ For all who rely on works of the law are under a curse; for it is written, "Cursed be everyone who does not abide by all things written in the Book of the Law, and do them."

¹¹ Now it is evident that no one is justified before God by the law, for "The righteous shall live by faith."

¹² But the law is not of faith, rather "The one who does them shall live by them."

¹³ Christ redeemed us from the curse of the law by becoming a curse for us—for it is written, "Cursed is everyone who is hanged on a tree"—

¹⁴ so that in Christ Jesus the blessing of Abraham might come to the Gentiles, so that we might

---

10. Cursed A citation of Deuteronomy 27:26: "'Cursed be anyone who does not confirm the words of this law by doing them.'"

They are cursed because of a person's inability to do "all things" according to the Law. The Law does not offer hope. James 2:10 echoes this: "For whoever keeps the whole law but fails in one point has become accountable for all of it." Faith, however, does offer hope.

11. A citation of Habakuk 2:4: "Behold, his soul is puffed up; it is not upright within him, but the righteous shall live by his faith."

12. A citation of Leviticus 18:5: "You shall therefore keep my statutes and my rules; if a person does them, he shall live by them: I am the Lord."

who does them shall live by them I.e., in contrast to merely believing in the law, one must actually live by it—all of it.

Hogg and Vine observe about the law: "Law is unbending, it yields nothing to weakness, its standard is never lowered, not even by a hairbreadth; law makes no compromise, and finds no room for mercy" (p. 83). The law by nature is the anthesis of faith and grace. It's a good thing for us the requirement for our salvation is faith rather than works!

13. A citation of Deuteronomy 21:23: "His body shall not remain all night on the tree, but you shall bury him the same day, for a hanged man is cursed by God. You shall not defile your land that the Lord your God is giving you for an inheritance."

the curse of the law The law's unbending nature, its curse, was fully met and fulfilled by Christ. This verse brings to mind 2 Corinthians 5:21: "For our sake he made him to be sin who knew no sin, so that in him we might become the righteousness of God."

receive the promised Spirit through faith.

15 ¶ To give a human example, brothers: even with a man-made covenant, no one annuls it or adds to it once it has been ratified.

16 Now the promises were made to Abraham and to his offspring. It does not say, "And to offsprings," referring to many, but referring to one, "And to your offspring," who is Christ.

17 This is what I mean: the law, which came 430 years afterward, does not annul a covenant previously ratified by God, so as to make the promise void.

18 For if the inheritance comes by the law, it no longer comes by promise; but God gave it to Abraham by a promise.

19 ¶ Why then the law? It was added because of transgressions, until the offspring should come to whom the promise had been made, and it was put in place through angels by an intermediary.

---

16. A citation of Genesis 22:17–18: "I will surely bless you, and I will surely multiply your offspring as the stars of heaven and as the sand that is on the seashore. And your offspring shall possess the gate of his enemies, and in your offspring shall all the nations of the earth be blessed, because you have obeyed my voice."

That Jesus' lineage goes back to Abraham is well-documented in the genealogical prologues of both Matthew and Luke (Matthew 1:1–17 and Luke 3:21–38). The Gospel of Matthew's first words are "The book of the genealogy of Jesus Christ, the son of David, the son of Abraham" (1:1).

18. A promise is dependent upon and accepted by faith; an inheritance is a legal matter and does not require faith, only the enforcement of the law.

19. It was added A reminder: the promise (faith) came first, to Abraham; the Law (works) came second, to Moses on Mt. Sinai.

See 1 Timothy 1:8–9a: "Now we know that the law is good, if one uses it lawfully, understanding this, that the law is not laid down for the just but for the lawless and disobedient, for the ungodly and sinners . . ."

I have heard the law explained this way: it is like a dentist's mirror. The mirror itself cannot correct or fix anything; its job is merely to illuminate any problems.

the offspring Jesus, referring back to verse 16.

put in place through angels Attested to in Acts 7:53 (". . . you who received the law as delivered by angels . . .") and Hebrews 2:2 ("For since the message declared by angels proved to be reliable . . .").

by an intermediary Moses. The point is that God Himself made the promise directly to Abraham, while the Law used intermediaries (angels and Moses). Moses' role as intermediary is clear in Exodus 20:18–19: "Now when all the people saw the thunder and the flashes of lightning and the sound of the trumpet and the mountain smoking, the

20 Now an intermediary implies more than one, but God is one.

21 ¶ Is the law then contrary to the promises of God? Certainly not! For if a law had been given that could give life, then righteousness would indeed be by the law.

22 But the Scripture imprisoned everything under sin, so that the promise by faith in Jesus Christ might be given to those who believe.

23 ¶ Now before faith came, we were held captive under the law, imprisoned until the coming faith would be revealed.

24 So then, the law was our guardian until Christ came, in order that we might be justified by faith.

25 But now that faith has come, we are no longer under a guardian,

26 for in Christ Jesus you are all sons of God, through faith.

27 For as many of you as were baptized into Christ have put on Christ.

28 There is neither Jew nor Greek, there is neither slave nor free, there is neither male nor female, for you are all one in Christ Jesus.

---

people were afraid and trembled, and they stood far off and said to Moses, 'You speak to us, and we will listen; but do not let God speak to us, lest we die.'"

21. then righteousness would indeed be by the law But we know from his previous arguments that righteousness cannot come by the law, so therefore there is no law that can give life. The law does not promise or give life. Only the promise of God—which, being a promise, by definition can therefore only be received by faith—can give life.

24. guardian In ancient Rome there were special slaves whose job was to take children to school and make sure they behaved. They were not teachers, but merely guides or guardians. Their title was "pedagogue" (*ped* meaning child, *gogue* meaning leader). This is the word Paul used to describe the Law that is here translated "guardian."

The pedagogue's job was two-fold according to Barnes' Notes and others—to keep the boys out of trouble and to lead them to the teacher. So, too, with the law. Its job is to keep us out of trouble and ultimately to lead us to the Teacher.

28. Similar to Romans 10:12 ("For there is no distinction between Jew and Greek; the same Lord is Lord of all, bestowing his riches on all who call on him") as well as 1 Corinthians 12:13 ("For in one Spirit we were all baptized into one body—Jews or Greeks, slaves or free—and all were made to drink of one Spirit").

²⁹ And if you are Christ's, then you are Abraham's offspring, heirs according to promise.

---

4 ¶ I MEAN THAT the heir, as long as he is a child, is no different from a slave, though he is the owner of everything,

² but he is under guardians and managers until the date set by his father.

³ In the same way we also, when we were children, were enslaved to the elementary principles of the world.

⁴ But when the fullness of time had come, God sent forth his Son, born of woman, born under the law,

⁵ to redeem those who were under the law, so that we might receive adoption as sons.

⁶ And because you are sons, God has sent the Spirit of his Son into our hearts, crying, "Abba! Father!"

Notes on Chapter 4

Chapter Summary Paul continues his arguments from the previous chapter. With the advent of Christ and the new covenant, we are now made fully sons and daughters of God.

He entreats us not to go back to being mere children, enslaved by sin and a fearful obedience to rules and regulation.

He concludes the chapter by comparing us to Ishmael and Isaac, Abraham's two sons. Ishmael represents slavery to the law and was born to a slave; Isaac represents grace, given by God's promise, and was born to a free woman. (For the complete context, see Genesis 16, 17, and 21.)

1. The Living Bible renders this verse, "But remember this, that if a father dies and leaves great wealth for his little son, that child is not much better off than a slave until he grows up, even though he actually owns everything his father had."

4. the fullness of time The only other time this phrase is used in the Bible is Ephesians 1:10: "As a plan for the fullness of time, to unite all things in him, things in heaven and things on earth." In the Galatians verse it is referring back to verse 2 ("until the date set by his father"). We cannot fully understand God's timing this side of heaven, but we can be certain that it was and is perfect.

5. adoption Keener, p. 430, observes that in the Roman world adoption could take place at any age and "cancelled all previous debts and relationships, defining the new son wholly in terms of his new relationship to his father, whose heir he thus became." This gives a much stronger significance to the idea that we are "adopted" by God.

6. because you are sons We receive the Spirit because of our becoming children of God, which is by faith (see verse 5).

Abba! Father! "Abba" is the Aramaic equivalent of "pappa" or "dad." According to Vines, the words are to be read

7 So you are no longer a slave, but a son, and if a son, then an heir through God.

8 ¶ Formerly, when you did not know God, you were enslaved to those that by nature are not gods.

9 But now that you have come to know God, or rather to be known by God, how can you turn back again to the weak and worthless elementary principles of the world, whose slaves you want to be once more?

10 You observe days and months and seasons and years!

11 I am afraid I may have labored over you in vain.

12 ¶ Brothers, I entreat you, become as I am, for I also have become as you are. You did me no wrong.

13 You know it was because of a bodily ailment that I preached the gospel to you at first,

14 and though my condition was a trial to you, you did not scorn or despise me, but received me as an angel of God, as Christ Jesus.

---

together, as if "dad, our father." The significance is the familiarity of the term. God no longer sees us as servants or subjects, but as His own children.

This intimacy with the Father is virtually unknown in the Old Testament. Mark 14:36 shows Jesus using the same combination ("And [Jesus] said, 'Abba, Father, all things are possible for you. Remove this cup from me. Yet not what I will, but what you will.'" Note that Jesus' familiarity with His Father did not preclude His obedience toward Him.) God is both our dad who loves us and our father whom we are to obey. (It should be pointed out that, according to the ESV Study Bible, adults as well as children used the term "Abba" and "the claim that 'Abba' meant 'Daddy' is misleading and runs the risk of irreverence." Hence, I have used "Dad" as a more appropriate term of familiarity.)

Paul repeats the theme in Romans 8:15: "For you did not receive the spirit of slavery to fall back into fear, but you have received the Spirit of adoption as sons, by whom we cry, 'Abba! Father!'" It has been observed that slaves in Jewish culture were not allowed to use the title "Abba" for their owners. What a privilege that we, like Jesus and only because of Him, can call God our Father. (1 John 3:1: "See what kind of love the Father has given to us, that we should be called children of God; and so we are.")

13. bodily ailment When combined with verse 15 ("If possible, you would have gouged out your eyes and given them to me"), it appears that Paul's medical problem was an optical one. Furthermore, verse 6:11 can be interpreted as

15 What then has become of the blessing you felt? For I testify to you that, if possible, you would have gouged out your eyes and given them to me.

16 Have I then become your enemy by telling you the truth?

17 They make much of you, but for no good purpose. They want to shut you out, that you may make much of them.

18 It is always good to be made much of for a good purpose, and not only when I am present with you,

19 my little children, for whom I am again in the anguish of childbirth until Christ is formed in you!

20 I wish I could be present with you now and change my tone, for I am perplexed about you.

21 ❡ Tell me, you who desire to be under the law, do you not listen to the law?

22 For it is written that Abraham had two sons, one by a slave woman and one by a free woman.

23 But the son of the slave was born according to the flesh, while the son of the free woman was born through promise.

24 Now this may be interpreted allegorically:

---

another indication of an eye problem ("See with what large letters I am writing to you with my own hand").

15. eyes When combined with verse 13 ("You know it was because of a bodily ailment that I preached the gospel to you at first"), it would appear that Paul's medical problem was an optical one. Furthermore, verse 6:11 can be interpreted as another indication of an eye problem ("See with what large letters I am writing to you with my own hand.")

22. one by a slave woman refers to Hagar, Sarah's slave (for Hagar's story, see Genesis 16).

one by a free woman refers to Sarah (see Genesis 21).

23. While Paul's audience would have understood this allegory immediately, a modern reader might need some context. Abraham had been promised by God that he would be the progenitor of a great nation (Genesis 12:2: "And I will make of you a great nation, and I will bless you and make your name great, so that you will be a blessing."). However, rather than wait for God to fulfill His promise, Abraham and his wife Sarah sought to make the promise come true in these women are two covenants. One is from Mount Sinai, bearing children for slavery; she is Hagar.

25 Now Hagar is Mount Sinai in Arabia; she corresponds to the present Jerusalem, for she is in slavery with her children.

26 But the Jerusalem above is free, and she is our mother.

27 For it is written,

> "Rejoice, O barren one who
>   does not bear;
> break forth and cry aloud, you
>   who are not in labor!
> For the children of the
>   desolate one will be more
>   than those of the one
>   who has a husband."

28 ❡ Now you, brothers, like Isaac, are children of promise.

29 But just as at that time he who was born according to the flesh persecuted him who was born according to the Spirit, so also it is now.

30 But what does the Scripture say? "Cast out the slave woman and her son, for the son of the slave woman shall not inherit with the son of the free woman."

---

another way. Advancing in age and herself barren, Sarah suggested to her husband that he father a child with her slave Hagar. That son was Ishmael—born "according to the flesh." God, however, remained faithful and allowed Abraham and Sarah to have a son, Isaac—"born through promise"—even though Sarah was well beyond childbearing years when he was born.

27. A citation of Isaiah 54:1.

28. children of promise Like Isaac, whose birth was miraculous and supernatural, Christians are born "not of blood nor of the will of the flesh nor of the will of men, but of God" (John 1:13). "Promise" here refers not to potential but to the miraculous fulfillment of what God had promised.

30. A citation of Genesis 21:10: "So [Sarah] said to Abraham, 'Cast out this slave woman with her son, for the son of this slave woman shall not be heir with my son Isaac.'"

31 So, brothers, we are not children of the slave but of the free woman.

---

5 ❡ FOR FREEDOM CHRIST has set us free; stand firm therefore, and do not submit again to a yoke of slavery.

2 ❡ Look: I, Paul, say to you that if you accept circumcision, Christ will be of no advantage to you.

3 I testify again to every man who accepts circumcision that he is obligated to keep the whole law.

4 You are severed from Christ, you who would be justified by the law; you have fallen away from grace.

5 For through the Spirit, by faith, we ourselves

---

31. This ties back to Paul's point in 3:7 ("Know then that it is those of faith who are the sons of Abraham") and 3:29 ("If you are Christ's, then you are Abraham's offspring, heirs according to promise").

Notes on Chapter 5

Chapter Summary What a great chapter! It builds on the theme expressed in its first verse: Christianity is not about the negatives (the Law) but the positives (the Promise). In this chapter Paul focuses on the practical application of the theology expressed in the previous chapters (yet he still takes the opportunity to throw in some significant anti-works digs).

1. This is the key verse and theme of the whole book! Given the context, "freedom" here is not license to sin, but relief from a salvation based on merit. Here is how J. B. Phillips puts it in his translation: "Plant your feet firmly therefore within the freedom that Christ has won for us, and do not let yourselves be caught again in the shackles of slavery."

2. if you accept circumcision That is, if you accept circumcision as a condition of salvation. It is obvious that Paul does not oppose the act of circumcision, but objects adding anything to faith as the condition of salvation (which is what he is using circumcision as a symbol of). To add anything to faith—be it circumcision, church attendance, or morality—is to abrogate Christ's gift!

3. obligated to keep the whole law Echoed in James 2:10: "For whoever keeps the whole law but fails in one point has become accountable for all of it."

4. severed from Christ The KJV renders this, "Christ is become of no effect unto you," which is a good way of putting it. The Greek word means to render useless or to cancel. So, to make works the condition for salvation in effect renders Christ's work for you useless. After all, grace and works are opposites and by definition cancel each other out.

fallen away from grace Lewis Sperry Chafer in his book *Salvation*, had this to say about this passage: "It is simply departing from the liberty wherewith Christ hath set us free. It is returning to the yoke and bondage of the law from which the death of Christ hath delivered us." In other words, he sees "falling from grace" not as a matter of losing one's eagerly wait for the hope of righteousness.

6 For in Christ Jesus neither circumcision nor uncircumcision counts for anything, but only faith working through love.

7 You were running well. Who hindered you from obeying the truth?

8 This persuasion is not from him who calls you.

9 A little leaven leavens the whole lump.

10 I have confidence in the Lord that you will take no other view than mine, and the one who is troubling you will bear the penalty, whoever he is.

11 But if I, brothers, still preach circumcision, why am I still being persecuted? In that case the offense of the cross has been removed.

12 I wish those who unsettle you would emasculate themselves!

---

salvation, but getting sucked back into a works-based relationship with God.

If the ESV rendering of this verse is correct, it paints a vivid picture: those who add works as a condition of salvation cut themselves off from Christ and fall away from the gospel of grace. Compare the lack of security of a works-based relationship with God with that described by Paul in Romans 5:2: "Through [Christ] we have also obtained access by faith into this grace in which we stand, and we rejoice in hope of the glory of God."

6. This is the first time the word *love* is mentioned in Galatians. It will be mentioned three more times, all in this chapter (verses 13, 14, and 22). Paul clearly wants to get our theology straight before calling us to live it out through love. Indeed, the security which comes from understanding our salvation allows us to love others more.

7–12. Paul addresses specifically those who have been propagating the message of works-based salvation, culminating in his vivid insult in verse 12.

8. not from him who calls you That is, God. Jesus tells us in John 6:44 that "no one can come to me unless the Father who sent me draws him."

9. Two possible reasons for Paul's inclusion of this proverbial expression are that false teaching among a few will quickly spread to the many, or that giving in on one principle—even circumcision—will lead to the destruction of grace. Paul also used this phrase in 1 Corinthians 5:6: "Your boasting is not good. Do you not know that a little leaven leavens the whole lump?"

11. Here's how The Living Bible renders this verse: "Some people even say that I myself am preaching that circumcision and Jewish laws are necessary to the plan of salvation. Well, if I preached that, I would be persecuted no more—for that message doesn't offend anyone. The fact that I am still being persecuted proves that I am still preaching salvation through faith in the cross of Christ alone."

12. emasculate themselves Paul's disgust and frustration with those who have led the Galatians astray leads him

_____

_____

_____

_____

_____

_____

_____

_____

_____

_____

_____

_____

_____

_____

_____

_____

_____

_____

¹³ ¶ For you were called to freedom, brothers. Only do not use your freedom as an opportunity for the flesh, but through love serve one another.

¹⁴ For the whole law is fulfilled in one word: "You shall love your neighbor as yourself."

¹⁵ But if you bite and devour one another, watch out that you are not consumed by one another.

¹⁶ ¶ But I say, walk by the Spirit, and you will not gratify the desires of the flesh.

¹⁷ For the desires of the flesh are against the Spirit, and the desires of the Spirit are against the flesh, for these are opposed to each other, to keep you from doing the things you want to do.

¹⁸ But if you are led by the Spirit, you are not under the law.

¹⁹ Now the works of the flesh are evident: sexual

---

to say in effect, "Don't stop at the foreskin, I wish you would go ahead and castrate yourself." Perhaps he meant it further to mean that to believe in the Law (versus Grace) is to emasculate and render powerless the message of the cross.

13. Here Paul tackles what is to this day the most commonly used objection to the gospel of grace: that it promotes antinomianism (that is, that the Christian has no obligation to adhere to the law). Consistently, as in this verse, Paul encourages us to live for and in obedience to God. But now the emphasis is on the law of Christ as opposed to the Old Testament law (6:2: "Bear one another's burdens, and so fulfill the law of Christ").

14. one word Here, "word" means a single precept or commandment, not a literal single word. Used similarly in Romans 13:9 ("The commandments, 'You shall not commit adultery, You shall not murder, You shall not steal, You shall not covet,' and any other commandment, are summed up in this word: 'You shall love your neighbor as yourself.'").

Paul is quoting Leviticus 19:18 ("You shall not take vengeance or bear a grudge against the songs of your own people, but you shall love your neighbor as yourself: I am the LORD.") Jesus also said it in Mark 12:31 ("The second is this: 'You shall love your neighbor as yourself.' There is no other commandment greater than these.")

16. This is the summary "practical" verse in the book. Verse 1 of this chapter summed up the theological argument ("For freedom Christ has set us free; stand firm therefore, and do not submit again to a yoke of slavery."). This verse now sums up how we are to apply the theology of grace. This is one of the great principles of Christian living. It puts it in positive mode. In *He That is Spiritual*, p. 96, Lewis Sperry Chafer put it, "The Spirit will do the walking in the Christian."

Whereas in the Old Testament God's people were encouraged to "walk by the law" (Leviticus 26:3–4: "If you walk in my statues and observe my commandments and do them, then I will give you your rains in their season ...") now we are to "walk by the Spirit."

18. The great British preacher J. R. W. Stott in his book, *The Cross of Christ* (p. 241) comments about this verse: "It emphatically does not mean that there are no moral absolutes ... or that we now have no obligation to obey God's law. [But] the law no longer enslaves us by its condemnation."

19–23. The Law = "do not." Grace = "do."

immorality, impurity, sensuality,

20 idolatry, sorcery, enmity, strife, jealousy, fits of anger, rivalries, dissensions, divisions,

21 envy, drunkenness, orgies, and things like these. I warn you, as I warned you before, that those who do such things will not inherit the kingdom of God.

22 But the fruit of the Spirit is love, joy, peace, patience, kindness, goodness, faithfulness,

23 gentleness, self-control; against such things there is no law.

24 And those who belong to Christ Jesus have crucified the flesh with its passions and desires.

25 ¶ If we live by the Spirit, let us also walk by the Spirit.

26 Let us not become conceited, provoking one another, envying one another.

6 ¶ BROTHERS, IF ANYONE is caught in any transgression, you who are spiritual should restore him in a spirit of gentleness. Keep watch on yourself, lest you too be tempted.

2 Bear one another's burdens, and so fulfill the

---

24. The key to how to crucify the flesh is found in the next verse.

26. This verse would probably fit better in the next chapter. Since chapter divisions were not added to the Bible until the 1200s and are not themselves part of the divine, inerrant word of God, it is very possible that this verse is the start of Paul's next point, which finishes five verses later.

Notes on Chapter 6

Chapter Summary This chapter continues Paul's practical application of the doctrine of grace, followed by a short return to his anti-works theme.

1. you who are spiritual That is, those walking by the Spirit as he just mentioned two verses previously.

a spirit of gentleness A wonderful and important reminder that while we are called to correct others, we should do so with humility. As Paul points out, you, too, might be tempted, and (in verse 3), we are "nothing."

In 1 Peter 3:15, Peter admonishes us to treat non-Christians "with gentleness and respect." Obviously the Christian attitude is never to lord one's position over someone else, but to treat them as equals in the eyes of God.

law of Christ.

³ For if anyone thinks he is something, when he is nothing, he deceives himself.

⁴ But let each one test his own work, and then his reason to boast will be in himself alone and not in his neighbor.

⁵ For each will have to bear his own load.

⁶ ¶ One who is taught the word must share all good things with the one who teaches.

⁷ Do not be deceived: God is not mocked, for whatever one sows, that will he also reap.

⁸ For the one who sows to his own flesh will from the flesh reap corruption, but the one who sows to the Spirit will from the Spirit reap eternal life.

⁹ And let us not grow weary of doing good, for in due season we will reap, if we do not give up.

¹⁰ So then, as we have opportunity, let us do good to everyone, and especially to those who are of the household of faith.

¹¹ ¶ See with what large letters I am writing to

---

2. law of Christ While he almost certainly uses this phrase to refer to the lordship of Christ and obedience to all of His teachings, Jesus did give one very specific command which could therefore be termed "the law of Christ": "A new commandment I give to you, that you love one another: just as I have loved you, you also are to love one another" (John 13:34).

The only other time Paul uses the phrase "law of Christ" is in 1 Corinthians 9:21: "To those outside the law I became as one outside the law (not being outside the law of God but under the law of Christ) that I might win those outside the law."

3. This is consistent with Paul's teaching in Romans 12:3: "For by the grace given to me I say to everyone among you not to think of himself more highly than he ought to think, but to think with sober judgement, each according to the measure of faith that God has assigned."

6. A favorite verse of ministers everywhere! Paul also shared this sentiment in 1 Corinthians 9:11: "If we have sown spiritual things among you, is it too much if we reap material things from you?"

7–8. Perhaps this is a restatement of Romans 6:23 ("For the wages of sin is death, but the free gift of God is eternal life in Christ Jesus our Lord." That is to say, if you want to use works to be saved, you will get what you deserve, and only that. But eternal life is a gift from God. (Some see verses 7 and 8 as culminating the edict in verse 6, not as Paul returning to the major theme of the letter.)

11. This is most commonly understood to mean that Paul used an amanuensis to transcribe the letter and has now taken you with my own hand.

12 It is those who want to make a good showing in the flesh who would force you to be circumcised, and only in order that they may not be persecuted for the cross of Christ.

13 For even those who are circumcised do not themselves keep the law, but they desire to have you circumcised that they may boast in your flesh.

14 But far be it from me to boast except in the cross of our Lord Jesus Christ, by which the world has been crucified to me, and I to the world.

15 For neither circumcision counts for anything, nor uncircumcision, but a new creation.

16 And as for all who walk by this rule, peace and mercy be upon them, and upon the Israel of God.

---

pen in hand personally to finish the missive. 2 Thessalonians 3:17 supports this thought ("I, Paul, write this greeting with my own hand. This is the sign of genuineness in every letter of mine; it is the way I write.").

large letters This could refer to distinctive handwriting on Paul's part (see the reference just cited to 2 Thessalonians 3:17), or it could be evidence of Paul's previously mentioned eye trouble (4:15: "...if possible, you would have gouged out your eyes and given them to me.").

Contextually, he seems to be saying of his conclusion: THIS IS IMPORTANT! Evidence of this is that he uses the next five verses to summarize the entire letter.

10. Perhaps this admonition gave rise to John Wesley's motto: "Do all the good you can, by all the means you can, in all the ways you can, in all the places you can, at all the times you can, to all the people you can, as long as ever you can."

13–14. To understand them, these verses should be read as one thought. The world is full of people who want to mix salvation with behavior, grace with works. Those who do so are only putting a band-aid on the real problem, which is a sinful heart and condition. But, as Paul points out here, it makes them look good (even though they themslves are not free from behavioral sin).

15. This is an echo of 5:6 ("For in Christ Jesus neither circumcision nor uncircumcision counts for anything, but only faith working through love."). As to the "new creation," 2 Corinthians 5:17 says, "Therefore, if anyone is in Christ, he is a new creation."

16. and ... the Israel of God While at first glance one might think this means the church (3:7: "Know then that it is those of faith who are the sons of Abraham," and 3:29: "And if you are Christ's, then you are Abraham's offspring, heirs according to promise."), the use of the word "and" indicates a separate group from "all who walk by this rule." Some have suggested Paul means Jewish Christians. (Romans 9:6–7 would be an example of when Paul made a distinction between Jews who believed in Christ and those who did not: "For not all who are descended from Israel belong to Israel, and not all are children of Abraham because they are his offspring.")

17 ❡ From now on let no one cause me trouble, for I bear on my body the marks of Jesus.

18 ❡ The grace of our Lord Jesus Christ be with your spirit, brothers. Amen.

17. the marks of Jesus Perhaps continuing with his circumcision metaphor, Paul brings up his own scars received in the service of Christ. He elaborates on those in 2 Corinthians 11:24–25 ("Five times I received at the hands of the Jews the forty lashes less one. Three times I was beaten with rods. Once I was stoned.").

18. Paul ends what has sometimes been a contentious letter with a note of grace and fellowship.

Galatians

without notes

---

1 PAUL, AN APOSTLE—NOT from men nor through man, but through Jesus Christ and God the Father, who raised him from the dead—

2 and all the brothers who are with me, ❡ To the churches of Galatia:

3 ❡ Grace to you and peace from God our Father and the Lord Jesus Christ,

4 who gave himself for our sins to deliver us from the present evil age, according to the will of our God and Father,

5 to whom be the glory forever and ever. Amen.

6 ❡ I am astonished that you are so quickly deserting him who called you in the grace of Christ and are turning to a different gospel—

7 not that there is another one, but there are some who trouble you and want to distort the gospel of Christ.

8 But even if we or an angel from heaven should preach to you a gospel contrary to the one we preached to you, let him be accursed.

9 As we have said before, so now I say again: If anyone is preaching to you a gospel contrary to the one you received, let him be accursed.

10 ¶ For am I now seeking the approval of man, or of God? Or am I trying to please man? If I were still trying to please man, I would not be a servant of Christ.

11 ¶ For I would have you know, brothers, that the gospel that was preached by me is not man's gospel.

12 For I did not receive it from any man, nor was I taught it, but I received it through a revelation of Jesus Christ.

13 For you have heard of my former life in Judaism, how I persecuted the church of God violently and tried to destroy it.

14 And I was advancing in Judaism beyond many of my own age among my people, so extremely zealous was I for the traditions of my fathers.

15 But when he who had set me apart before I was born, and who called me by his grace,

16 was pleased to reveal his Son to me, in order that I might preach him among the Gentiles, I did not immediately consult with anyone;

17 nor did I go up to Jerusalem to those who were apostles before me, but I went away into Arabia, and returned again to Damascus.

18 ¶ Then after three years I went up to Jerusalem to visit Cephas and remained with him fifteen days.

19 But I saw none of the other apostles except James the Lord's brother.

20 (In what I am writing to you, before God, I do not lie!)

21 Then I went into the regions of Syria and Cilicia.

22 And I was still unknown in person to the churches of Judea that are in Christ.

23 They only were hearing it said, "He who used to persecute us is now preaching the faith he once tried to destroy."

24 And they glorified God because of me.

---

2 ¶ THEN AFTER fourteen years I went up again to Jerusalem with Barnabas, taking Titus along with me.

2 I went up because of a revelation and set before them (though privately before those who seemed influential) the gospel that I proclaim among the Gentiles, in order to make sure I was not running or had not run in vain.

3 But even Titus, who was with me, was not forced to be circumcised, though he was a Greek.

4 Yet because of false brothers secretly brought in—who slipped in to spy out our freedom that we have in Christ Jesus, so that they might bring us into slavery—

5 to them we did not yield in submission even for a moment, so that the truth of the gospel might be preserved for you.

6 And from those who seemed to be influential (what they were makes no difference to me; God shows no partiality)—those, I say, who seemed influential added nothing to me.

7 On the contrary, when they saw that I had been entrusted with the gospel to the uncircumcised, just as Peter had been entrusted with the gospel to the circumcised

8 (for he who worked through Peter for his apostolic ministry to the circumcised worked also through me for mine to the Gentiles),

9 and when James and Cephas and John, who seemed to be pillars, perceived the grace that was given to me, they gave the right hand of fellowship to Barnabas and me, that we should go to the Gentiles and they to the circumcised.

10 Only, they asked us to remember the poor, the very thing I was eager to do.

11 ¶ But when Cephas came to Antioch, I opposed him to his face, because he stood condemned.

12 For before certain men came from James, he was eating with the Gentiles; but when they came he drew back and separated himself, fearing the circumcision party.

13 And the rest of the Jews acted hypocritically along with him, so that even Barnabas was led astray by their hypocrisy.

14 But when I saw that their conduct was not in step with the truth of the gospel, I said to Cephas before them all, "If you, though a Jew, live like a Gentile and not like a Jew, how can you force the Gentiles to live like Jews?"

15 We ourselves are Jews by birth and not Gentile sinners;

16 yet we know that a person is not justified by works of the law but through faith in Jesus Christ, so we also have believed in Christ Jesus, in order to be justified by faith in Christ and not by works of the law, because by works of the law no one will be justified.

17 But if, in our endeavor to be justified in Christ, we too were found to be sinners, is Christ then a servant of sin? Certainly not!

18 For if I rebuild what I tore down, I prove myself to be a transgressor.

19 For through the law I died to the law, so that I might live to God.

20 I have been crucified with Christ. It is no longer I who live, but Christ who lives in me. And the life I now live in the flesh I live by faith in the Son of God, who loved me and gave himself for me.

21 I do not nullify the grace of God, for if justification were through the law, then Christ died for no purpose.

---

3 ¶ O FOOLISH Galatians! Who has bewitched you? It was before your eyes that Jesus Christ was publicly portrayed as crucified.

2 Let me ask you only this: Did you receive the Spirit by works of the law or by hearing with faith?

3 Are you so foolish? Having begun by the Spirit, are you now being perfected by the flesh?

4 Did you suffer so many things in vain—if indeed it was in vain?

5 Does he who supplies the Spirit to you and works miracles among you do so by works of the law, or by hearing with faith—

6 just as Abraham "believed God, and it was counted to him as righteousness"?

7 Know then that it is those of faith who are the sons of Abraham.

8 And the Scripture, foreseeing that God would justify the Gentiles by faith, preached the gospel beforehand to Abraham, saying, "In you shall all the nations be blessed."

9 So then, those who are of faith are blessed along with Abraham, the man of faith.

10 ¶ For all who rely on works of the law are under a curse; for it is written, "Cursed be everyone who does not abide by all things written in the Book of the Law, and do them."

11 Now it is evident that no one is justified before God by the law, for "The righteous shall live by faith."

12 But the law is not of faith, rather "The one who does them shall live by them."

13 Christ redeemed us from the curse of the law by becoming a curse for us—for it is written, "Cursed is everyone who is hanged on a tree"—

14 so that in Christ Jesus the blessing of Abraham might come to the Gentiles, so that we might receive the promised Spirit through faith.

15 ❡ To give a human example, brothers: even with a man-made covenant, no one annuls it or adds to it once it has been ratified.

16 Now the promises were made to Abraham and to his offspring. It does not say, "And to offsprings," referring to many, but referring to one, "And to your offspring," who is Christ.

17 This is what I mean: the law, which came 430 years afterward, does not annul a covenant previously ratified by God, so as to make the promise void.

18 For if the inheritance comes by the law, it no longer comes by promise; but God gave it to Abraham by a promise.

19 ❡ Why then the law? It was added because of transgressions, until the offspring should come to whom the promise had been made, and it was put in place through angels by an intermediary.

20 Now an intermediary implies more than one, but God is one.

21 ❡ Is the law then contrary to the promises of God? Certainly not! For if a law had been given that could give life, then righteousness would indeed be by the law.

22 But the Scripture imprisoned everything

under sin, so that the promise by faith in Jesus Christ might be given to those who believe.

23 ❡ Now before faith came, we were held captive under the law, imprisoned until the coming faith would be revealed.

24 So then, the law was our guardian until Christ came, in order that we might be justified by faith.

25 But now that faith has come, we are no longer under a guardian,

26 for in Christ Jesus you are all sons of God, through faith.

27 For as many of you as were baptized into Christ have put on Christ.

28 There is neither Jew nor Greek, there is neither slave nor free, there is neither male nor female, for you are all one in Christ Jesus.

29 And if you are Christ's, then you are Abraham's offspring, heirs according to promise.

4 ❡ I MEAN that the heir, as long as he is a child, is no different from a slave, though he is the owner of everything,

2 but he is under guardians and managers until the date set by his father.

3 In the same way we also, when we were children, were enslaved to the elementary principles of the world.

4 But when the fullness of time had come, God sent forth his Son, born of woman, born under the law,

5 to redeem those who were under the law, so that we might receive adoption as sons.

6 And because you are sons, God has sent the Spirit of his Son into our hearts, crying, "Abba! Father!"

7 So you are no longer a slave, but a son, and if a son, then an heir through God.

8 ¶ Formerly, when you did not know God, you were enslaved to those that by nature are not gods.

9 But now that you have come to know God, or rather to be known by God, how can you turn back again to the weak and worthless elementary principles of the world, whose slaves you want to be once more?

10 You observe days and months and seasons and years!

11 I am afraid I may have labored over you in vain.

12 ¶ Brothers, I entreat you, become as I am, for I also have become as you are. You did me no wrong.

13 You know it was because of a bodily ailment that I preached the gospel to you at first,

14 and though my condition was a trial to you, you did not scorn or despise me, but received me as an angel of God, as Christ Jesus.

15 What then has become of the blessing you felt? For I testify to you that, if possible, you would have gouged out your eyes and given them to me.

16 Have I then become your enemy by telling you the truth?

17 They make much of you, but for no good purpose. They want to shut you out, that you may make much of them.

18 It is always good to be made much of for a good purpose, and not only when I am present with you,

19 my little children, for whom I am again in the

anguish of childbirth until Christ is formed in you!

20 I wish I could be present with you now and change my tone, for I am perplexed about you.

21 ❡ Tell me, you who desire to be under the law, do you not listen to the law?

22 For it is written that Abraham had two sons, one by a slave woman and one by a free woman.

23 But the son of the slave was born according to the flesh, while the son of the free woman was born through promise.

24 Now this may be interpreted allegorically: these women are two covenants. One is from Mount Sinai, bearing children for slavery; she is Hagar.

25 Now Hagar is Mount Sinai in Arabia; she corresponds to the present Jerusalem, for she is in slavery with her children.

26 But the Jerusalem above is free, and she is our mother.

27 For it is written,

> "Rejoice, O barren one who
>   does not bear;
>
> break forth and cry aloud, you
>   who are not in labor!
>
> For the children of the
>   desolate one will be more
>   than those of the one
>   who has a husband."

28 ❡ Now you, brothers, like Isaac, are children of promise.

29 But just as at that time he who was born according to the flesh persecuted him who was born according to the Spirit, so also it is now.

30 But what does the Scripture say? "Cast out the slave woman and her son, for the son of the slave woman shall not inherit with the son of the free woman."

31 So, brothers, we are not children of the slave but of the free woman.

---

5 ¶ FOR FREEDOM Christ has set us free; stand firm therefore, and do not submit again to a yoke of slavery.

2 ¶ Look: I, Paul, say to you that if you accept circumcision, Christ will be of no advantage to you.

3 I testify again to every man who accepts circumcision that he is obligated to keep the whole law.

4 You are severed from Christ, you who would be justified by the law; you have fallen away from grace.

5 For through the Spirit, by faith, we ourselves eagerly wait for the hope of righteousness.

6 For in Christ Jesus neither circumcision nor uncircumcision counts for anything, but only faith working through love.

7 You were running well. Who hindered you from obeying the truth?

8 This persuasion is not from him who calls you.

9 A little leaven leavens the whole lump.

10 I have confidence in the Lord that you will take no other view than mine, and the one who is troubling you will bear the penalty, whoever he is.

11 But if I, brothers, still preach circumcision, why am I still being persecuted? In that case the offense of the cross has been removed.

12 I wish those who unsettle you would emasculate themselves!

13 ¶ For you were called to freedom, brothers. Only do not use your freedom as an opportunity for the flesh, but through love serve one another.

14 For the whole law is fulfilled in one word: "You shall love your neighbor as yourself."

15 But if you bite and devour one another, watch out that you are not consumed by one another.

16 ¶ But I say, walk by the Spirit, and you will not gratify the desires of the flesh.

17 For the desires of the flesh are against the Spirit, and the desires of the Spirit are against the flesh, for these are opposed to each other, to keep you from doing the things you want to do.

18 But if you are led by the Spirit, you are not under the law.

19 Now the works of the flesh are evident: sexual immorality, impurity, sensuality,

20 idolatry, sorcery, enmity, strife, jealousy, fits of anger, rivalries, dissensions, divisions,

21 envy, drunkenness, orgies, and things like these. I warn you, as I warned you before, that those who do such things will not inherit the kingdom of God.

22 But the fruit of the Spirit is love, joy, peace, patience, kindness, goodness, faithfulness,

23 gentleness, self-control; against such things there is no law.

24 And those who belong to Christ Jesus have crucified the flesh with its passions and desires.

25 ¶ If we live by the Spirit, let us also walk by

the Spirit.

26 Let us not become conceited, provoking one another, envying one another.

6 ¶ Brothers, if anyone is caught in any transgression, you who are spiritual should restore him in a spirit of gentleness. Keep watch on yourself, lest you too be tempted.

2 Bear one another's burdens, and so fulfill the law of Christ.

3 For if anyone thinks he is something, when he is nothing, he deceives himself.

4 But let each one test his own work, and then his reason to boast will be in himself alone and not in his neighbor.

5 For each will have to bear his own load.

---

6 ¶ ONE WHO is taught the word must share all good things with the one who teaches.

7 Do not be deceived: God is not mocked, for whatever one sows, that will he also reap.

8 For the one who sows to his own flesh will from the flesh reap corruption, but the one who sows to the Spirit will from the Spirit reap eternal life.

9 And let us not grow weary of doing good, for in due season we will reap, if we do not give up.

10 So then, as we have opportunity, let us do good to everyone, and especially to those who are of the household of faith.

11 ¶ See with what large letters I am writing to you with my own hand.

12 It is those who want to make a good showing in the flesh who would force you to be circumcised, and only in order that they may not be persecuted for the cross of Christ.

13 For even those who are circumcised do not themselves keep the law, but they desire to have you circumcised that they may boast in your flesh.

14 But far be it from me to boast except in the cross of our Lord Jesus Christ, by which the world has been crucified to me, and I to the world.

15 For neither circumcision counts for anything, nor uncircumcision, but a new creation.

16 And as for all who walk by this rule, peace and mercy be upon them, and upon the Israel of God.

17 ¶ From now on let no one cause me trouble, for I bear on my body the marks of Jesus.

18 ¶ The grace of our Lord Jesus Christ be with your spirit, brothers. Amen.

Appendix B

Galatians

King James Version

---

1 PAUL, AN APOSTLE, (not of men, neither by man, but by Jesus Christ, and God the Father, who raised him from the dead;)

2 And all the brethren which are with me, unto the churches of Galatia:

3 Grace be to you and peace from God the Father, and from our Lord Jesus Christ,

4 Who gave himself for our sins, that he might deliver us from this present evil world, according to the will of God and our Father:

5 To whom be glory for ever and ever. Amen.

6 I marvel that ye are so soon removed from him that called you into the grace of Christ unto another gospel:

7 Which is not another; but there be some that trouble you, and would pervert the gospel of Christ.

8 But though we, or an angel from heaven, preach any other gospel unto you than that which we have preached unto you, let him be accursed.

9 As we said before, so say I now again, If any man preach any other gospel unto you than that ye have received, let him be accursed.

10 For do I now persuade men, or God? or do I seek to please men? for if I yet pleased men, I should not be the servant of Christ.

11 But I certify you, brethren, that the gospel which was preached of me is not after man.

12 For I neither received it of man, neither was I taught it, but by the revelation of Jesus Christ.

13 For ye have heard of my conversation in time past in the Jews' religion, how that beyond measure I persecuted the church of God, and wasted it:

14 And profited in the Jews' religion above many my equals in mine own nation, being more exceedingly zealous of the traditions of my fathers.

[15] But when it pleased God, who separated me from my mother's womb, and called me by his grace,

[16] To reveal his Son in me, that I might preach him among the heathen; immediately I conferred not with flesh and blood:

[17] Neither went I up to Jerusalem to them which were apostles before me; but I went into Arabia, and returned again unto Damascus.

[18] Then after three years I went up to Jerusalem to see Peter, and abode with him fifteen days.

[19] But other of the apostles saw I none, save James the Lord's brother.

[20] Now the things which I write unto you, behold, before God, I lie not.

[21] Afterwards I came into the regions of Syria and Cilicia;

[22] And was unknown by face unto the churches of Judaea which were in Christ:

[23] But they had heard only, That he which persecuted us in times past now preacheth the faith which once he destroyed.

[24] And they glorified God in me.

---

2 THEN FOURTEEN YEARS after I went up again to Jerusalem with Barnabas, and took Titus with me also.

[2] And I went up by revelation, and communicated unto them that gospel which I preach among the Gentiles, but privately to them which were of reputation, lest by any means I should run, or had run, in vain.

[3] But neither Titus, who was with me, being a Greek, was compelled to be circumcised:

[4] And that because of false brethren unawares brought in, who came in privily to spy out our liberty which we have in Christ Jesus, that they might bring us into bondage:

[5] To whom we gave place by subjection, no, not for an hour; that the truth of the gospel might continue with you.

[6] But of these who seemed to be somewhat, (whatsoever they were,

it maketh no matter to me: God accepteth no man's person:) for they who seemed to be somewhat in conference added nothing to me:

⁷ But contrariwise, when they saw that the gospel of the uncircumcision was committed unto me, as the gospel of the circumcision was unto Peter;

⁸ (For he that wrought effectually in Peter to the apostleship of the circumcision, the same was mighty in me toward the Gentiles:)

⁹ And when James, Cephas, and John, who seemed to be pillars, perceived the grace that was given unto me, they gave to me and Barnabas the right hands of fellowship; that we should go unto the heathen, and they unto the circumcision.

¹⁰ Only they would that we should remember the poor; the same which I also was forward to do.

¹¹ But when Peter was come to Antioch, I withstood him to the face, because he was to be blamed.

¹² For before that certain came from James, he did eat with the Gentiles: but when they were come, he withdrew and separated himself, fearing them which were of the circumcision.

¹³ And the other Jews dissembled likewise with him; insomuch that Barnabas also was carried away with their dissimulation.

¹⁴ But when I saw that they walked not uprightly according to the truth of the gospel, I said unto Peter before them all, If thou, being a Jew, livest after the manner of Gentiles, and not as do the Jews, why compellest thou the Gentiles to live as do the Jews?

¹⁵ We who are Jews by nature, and not sinners of the Gentiles,

¹⁶ Knowing that a man is not justified by the works of the law, but by the faith of Jesus Christ, even we have believed in Jesus Christ, that we might be justified by the faith of Christ, and not by the works of the law: for by the works of the law shall no flesh be justified.

¹⁷ But if, while we seek to be justified by Christ, we ourselves also are found sinners, is therefore Christ the minister of sin? God forbid.

¹⁸ For if I build again the things which I destroyed, I make myself a transgressor.

¹⁹ For I through the law am dead to the law, that I might live unto God.

20 I am crucified with Christ: nevertheless I live; yet not I, but Christ liveth in me: and the life which I now live in the flesh I live by the faith of the Son of God, who loved me, and gave himself for me.

21 I do not frustrate the grace of God: for if righteousness come by the law, then Christ is dead in vain.

---

3 O FOOLISH GALATIANS, who hath bewitched you, that ye should not obey the truth, before whose eyes Jesus Christ hath been evidently set forth, crucified among you?

2 This only would I learn of you, Received ye the Spirit by the works of the law, or by the hearing of faith?

3 Are ye so foolish? having begun in the Spirit, are ye now made perfect by the flesh?

4 Have ye suffered so many things in vain? if it be yet in vain.

5 He therefore that ministereth to you the Spirit, and worketh miracles among you, doeth he it by the works of the law, or by the hearing of faith?

6 Even as Abraham believed God, and it was accounted to him for righteousness.

7 Know ye therefore that they which are of faith, the same are the children of Abraham.

8 And the scripture, foreseeing that God would justify the heathen through faith, preached before the gospel unto Abraham, saying, In thee shall all nations be blessed.

9 So then they which be of faith are blessed with faithful Abraham.

10 For as many as are of the works of the law are under the curse: for it is written, Cursed is every one that continueth not in all things which are written in the book of the law to do them.

11 But that no man is justified by the law in the sight of God, it is evident: for, The just shall live by faith.

12 And the law is not of faith: but, The man that doeth them shall live in them.

13 Christ hath redeemed us from the curse of the law, being made a curse for us: for it is written, Cursed is every one that hangeth on a tree:

14 That the blessing of Abraham might come on the Gentiles through Jesus Christ; that we might receive the promise of the Spirit through faith.

15 Brethren, I speak after the manner of men; Though it be but a man's covenant, yet if it be confirmed, no man disannulleth, or addeth thereto.

16 Now to Abraham and his seed were the promises made. He saith not, And to seeds, as of many; but as of one, And to thy seed, which is Christ.

17 And this I say, that the covenant, that was confirmed before of God in Christ, the law, which was four hundred and thirty years after, cannot disannul, that it should make the promise of none effect.

18 For if the inheritance be of the law, it is no more of promise: but God gave it to Abraham by promise.

19 Wherefore then serveth the law? It was added because of transgressions, till the seed should come to whom the promise was made; and it was ordained by angels in the hand of a mediator.

20 Now a mediator is not a mediator of one, but God is one.

21 Is the law then against the promises of God? God forbid: for if there had been a law given which could have given life, verily righteousness should have been by the law.

22 But the scripture hath concluded all under sin, that the promise by faith of Jesus Christ might be given to them that believe.

23 But before faith came, we were kept under the law, shut up unto the faith which should afterwards be revealed.

24 Wherefore the law was our schoolmaster to bring us unto Christ, that we might be justified by faith.

25 But after that faith is come, we are no longer under a schoolmaster.

26 For ye are all the children of God by faith in Christ Jesus.

27 For as many of you as have been baptized into Christ have put on Christ.

28 There is neither Jew nor Greek, there is neither bond nor free, there is neither male nor female: for ye are all one in Christ Jesus.

29 And if ye be Christ's, then are ye Abraham's seed, and heirs according to the promise.

---

4 Now I SAY, That the heir, as long as he is a child, differeth nothing from a servant, though he be lord of all;

2 But is under tutors and governors until the time appointed of the father.

3 Even so we, when we were children, were in bondage under the elements of the world:

4 But when the fulness of the time was come, God sent forth his Son, made of a woman, made under the law,

5 To redeem them that were under the law, that we might receive the adoption of sons.

6 And because ye are sons, God hath sent forth the Spirit of his Son into your hearts, crying, Abba, Father.

7 Wherefore thou art no more a servant, but a son; and if a son, then an heir of God through Christ.

8 Howbeit then, when ye knew not God, ye did service unto them which by nature are no gods.

9 But now, after that ye have known God, or rather are known of God, how turn ye again to the weak and beggarly elements, whereunto ye desire again to be in bondage?

10 Ye observe days, and months, and times, and years.

11 I am afraid of you, lest I have bestowed upon you labour in vain.

12 Brethren, I beseech you, be as I am; for I am as ye are: ye have not injured me at all.

13 Ye know how through infirmity of the flesh I preached the gospel unto you at the first.

14 And my temptation which was in my flesh ye despised not, nor rejected; but received me as an angel of God, even as Christ Jesus.

15 Where is then the blessedness ye spake of? for I bear you record, that, if it had been possible, ye would have plucked out your own eyes, and have given them to me.

¹⁶ Am I therefore become your enemy, because I tell you the truth?

¹⁷ They zealously affect you, but not well; yea, they would exclude you, that ye might affect them.

¹⁸ But it is good to be zealously affected always in a good thing, and not only when I am present with you.

¹⁹ My little children, of whom I travail in birth again until Christ be formed in you,

²⁰ I desire to be present with you now, and to change my voice; for I stand in doubt of you.

²¹ Tell me, ye that desire to be under the law, do ye not hear the law?

²² For it is written, that Abraham had two sons, the one by a bond-maid, the other by a freewoman.

²³ But he who was of the bondwoman was born after the flesh; but he of the freewoman was by promise.

²⁴ Which things are an allegory: for these are the two covenants; the one from the mount Sinai, which gendereth to bondage, which is Agar.

²⁵ For this Agar is mount Sinai in Arabia, and answereth to Jerusalem which now is, and is in bondage with her children.

²⁶ But Jerusalem which is above is free, which is the mother of us all.

²⁷ For it is written, Rejoice, thou barren that bearest not; break forth and cry, thou that travailest not: for the desolate hath many more children than she which hath an husband.

²⁸ Now we, brethren, as Isaac was, are the children of promise.

²⁹ But as then he that was born after the flesh persecuted him that was born after the Spirit, even so it is now.

³⁰ Nevertheless what saith the scripture? Cast out the bondwoman and her son: for the son of the bondwoman shall not be heir with the son of the freewoman.

³¹ So then, brethren, we are not children of the bondwoman, but of the free.

5 STAND FAST THEREFORE in the liberty wherewith Christ hath made us free, and be not entangled again with the yoke of bondage.

2 Behold, I Paul say unto you, that if ye be circumcised, Christ shall profit you nothing.

3 For I testify again to every man that is circumcised, that he is a debtor to do the whole law.

4 Christ is become of no effect unto you, whosoever of you are justified by the law; ye are fallen from grace.

5 For we through the Spirit wait for the hope of righteousness by faith.

6 For in Jesus Christ neither circumcision availeth anything, nor uncircumcision; but faith which worketh by love.

7 Ye did run well; who did hinder you that ye should not obey the truth?

8 This persuasion cometh not of him that calleth you.

9 A little leaven leaveneth the whole lump.

10 I have confidence in you through the Lord, that ye will be none otherwise minded: but he that troubleth you shall bear his judgment, whosoever he be.

11 And I, brethren, if I yet preach circumcision, why do I yet suffer persecution? then is the offence of the cross ceased.

12 I would they were even cut off which trouble you.

13 For, brethren, ye have been called unto liberty; only use not liberty for an occasion to the flesh, but by love serve one another.

14 For all the law is fulfilled in one word, even in this; Thou shalt love thy neighbour as thyself.

15 But if ye bite and devour one another, take heed that ye be not consumed one of another.

16 This I say then, Walk in the Spirit, and ye shall not fulfil the lust of the flesh.

17 For the flesh lusteth against the Spirit, and the Spirit against the flesh: and these are contrary the one to the other: so that ye cannot do the things that ye would.

18 But if ye be led of the Spirit, ye are not under the law.

19 Now the works of the flesh are manifest, which are these; Adultery, fornication, uncleanness, lasciviousness,

20 Idolatry, witchcraft, hatred, variance, emulations, wrath, strife, seditions, heresies,

21 Envyings, murders, drunkenness, revellings, and such like: of the which I tell you before, as I have also told you in time past, that they which do such things shall not inherit the kingdom of God.

22 But the fruit of the Spirit is love, joy, peace, longsuffering, gentleness, goodness, faith,

23 Meekness, temperance: against such there is no law.

24 And they that are Christ's have crucified the flesh with the affections and lusts.

25 If we live in the Spirit, let us also walk in the Spirit.

26 Let us not be desirous of vain glory, provoking one another, envying one another.

---

6 BRETHREN, IF A man be overtaken in a fault, ye which are spiritual, restore such an one in the spirit of meekness; considering thyself, lest thou also be tempted.

2 Bear ye one another's burdens, and so fulfil the law of Christ.

3 For if a man think himself to be something, when he is nothing, he deceiveth himself.

4 But let every man prove his own work, and then shall he have rejoicing in himself alone, and not in another.

5 For every man shall bear his own burden.

6 Let him that is taught in the word communicate unto him that teacheth in all good things.

7 Be not deceived; God is not mocked: for whatsoever a man soweth, that shall he also reap.

8 For he that soweth to his flesh shall of the flesh reap corruption; but he that soweth to the Spirit shall of the Spirit reap life everlasting.

9 And let us not be weary in well doing: for in due season we shall reap, if we faint not.

10 As we have therefore opportunity, let us do good unto all men, especially unto them who are of the household of faith.

11 Ye see how large a letter I have written unto you with mine own hand.

12 As many as desire to make a fair shew in the flesh, they constrain you to be circumcised; only lest they should suffer persecution for the cross of Christ.

13 For neither they themselves who are circumcised keep the law; but desire to have you circumcised, that they may glory in your flesh.

14 But God forbid that I should glory, save in the cross of our Lord Jesus Christ, by whom the world is crucified unto me, and I unto the world.

15 For in Christ Jesus neither circumcision availeth anything, nor uncircumcision, but a new creature.

16 And as many as walk according to this rule, peace be on them, and mercy, and upon the Israel of God.

17 From henceforth let no man trouble me: for I bear in my body the marks of the Lord Jesus.

18 Brethren, the grace of our Lord Jesus Christ be with your spirit. Amen.

Appendix C

Study Questions

Note: To help you answer these questions, use the annotations in this book as well as other study aids you may have. These questions can be used as either personal or group study questions.

Chapter 1

1. Who was Paul? What was his background? How was he converted?

2. Why is Paul's background and conversion important to the context of Galatians?

3. What is the gospel of grace that Paul is talking about?

4. What does Paul mean in verse 10, and how does that apply to your own life?

5. Where did Paul learn the gospel?

6. Who was Cephas? Why might Paul have been intimidated by him, and do you think he was?

7. See verse 24. Is anyone glorifying God because of you?

Chapter 2

1. How long had Paul been a Christian before the events described in this chapter?

2. What is circumcision? What does it mean, symbolically, in Galatians?

3. What is the central conflict of this chapter (and indeed, of the whole book)?

4. Put verse 16 in your own words.

5. What are some verses—outside of Galatians—that confirm Paul's argument?

6. Whom are we to live for now?

7. What is the argument Paul makes in verse 21?

Chapter 3
1. What does Paul mean in verse 1 that the Galatians have been "bewitched"?

2. What is the story of Abraham, and how is it related to faith?

3. According to verses 7–9, who are the true sons of Abraham?

4. What is the shortcoming of the law?

5. Discuss the legal argument Paul makes in verses 15–18.

6. Why did God give us the law?

7. What does "guardian" mean in verse 24?

8. What are the broad-ranging implications of verse 28?

Chapter 4
1. How does Paul describe (in verses 1–7) our new relationship with the Father? How does this relationship come into being?

2. What are some of the implications of the fact that believers are now heirs of God?

3. How do verses 8–11 fit into Paul's argument for grace?

4. What do you think Paul's physical ailment was?

5. What is the analogy that Paul is making when he speaks about Abraham's two sons?

6. Why, in your mind, is grace superior to the law?

7. What are some ways that Paul compares the law to enslavement in Galatians?

Chapter 5
1. Does verse 1 give us license to sin? If not, why not? That is, what do you think the point of the verse is?

2. What is circumcision a picture of in Galatians?

3. What does it mean to "fall from grace"?

4. According to verses 13–15, what is the result of grace supposed to be in our lives?

5. What does it mean to "walk by the Spirit"? Who is the Spirit?

6. What is the difference, if any, between walking by the Spirit and trying to do all the right things?

7. He contrasts two lists of things in verses 19–24. What are those two lists? Which is superior, and why?

8. What keeps us from walking by the Spirit?

Chapter 6

1. How should we approach a sinning brother?

2. What does it mean to "bear one another's burdens"?

3. What does verse 6 mean? What about verses 7–8?

4. What are some things that you can do to serve others?

5. What might the significance of "the large letters" he mentions in verse 11 be?

6. What seems to be the motivation of people pushing for good deeds (see verse 12)?

7. When's the last time you boasted to someone about what Christ has done for you?

Sources Cited

Barnes, Albert. *Barnes' Notes on the New Testament*. Grand Rapids, Michigan: Kregel Publications, 1980

Chafer, Lewis Sperry. *He That is Spiritual*. Grand Rapids, Michigan: Zondervan Publishing House, 1979

———. *Salvation*. Grand Rapids, Michigan: Zondervan Publishing House, 1980

Chamblin, Knox. "Pauline Epistles, Galatians." Reformed Theological Seminary, http://itunes.rts.edu/

Crossway Bibles. *The ESV Study Bible, English Standard Version*. Wheaton, Illinois: Crossway Bibles, 2008

Halley, Henry Hampton. *Halley's Bible Handbook with the New International Version*. Grand Rapids, Michigan: Zondervan Publishing House, 2000

Keener, Craig S. *The IVP Bible Background Commentary: New Testament*. Downers Grove, Illinois: InterVarsity Press, 1993

KNT Charitable Trust. *The Living Bible*. Wheaton, Illinois: Tyndale House Publishers, Inc., 1971

Ligonier Ministries. *The Reformation Study Bible: English Standard Version*. Edited by R. C. Sproul. Lake Mary, Florida, 2005

Mounce, William D. *Mounce's Complete Expository Dictionary of Old and New Testament Words*. Grand Rapids, Michigan: Zondervan Publishing House, 2006

Phillips, J. B. *The New Testament in Modern English: Student Edition*. New York, New York: The Macmillan Company, 1972

Ryrie, Charles Caldwell. *The Ryrie Study Bible: New American Standard Translation*. Chicago, Illinois: Moody Press, 1978

Stott, John R. W. *The Cross of Christ*. Downers Grove, Illinois: InterVarsity Press, 1986

Vine, W. E., with C. F. Hogg. *Vine's Expository Commentary on Galatians*. Nashville, Tennessee: Thomas Nelson Publishers, 1997

Zondervan Corporation. *The New Compact Bible Dictionary*. Edited by T. Alton Bryant. Grand Rapids, Michigan: Zondervan Publishing House, 1967

———. *The NIV Study Bible: 10th Anniversary Edition*. Edited by Kenneth Barker. Grand Rapids, Michigan: Zondervan Publishing House, 1995

www.ingramcontent.com/pod-product-compliance
Lightning Source LLC
Chambersburg PA
CBHW060041040426
42331CB00032B/1994